HOW TO
STOP LOSING
YOUR COOL

Definitive Guide to Master Your Emotions,
Increase Emotional Intelligence and Achieve
Freedom from Stress, Depression and Anger

HENRY W. BUKOWSKI

Book and Cover design: Raphael A.
Printed in the United States of America

First Edition : July 2020
Revised Edition : June 2022

DEDICATION

To my beloved wife Katherine

You never leave my mind. Never. Even when I have a
million things to think about.

CONTENTS

INTRODUCTION

I have a question for you. Why are you reading this book? If your answer is that you are simply taking time out from your idyllic life with no stress, no anger issues, and no anxiety, then please close this book, as it obviously is not for you.

However, if you are ready to take a hard and honest look at your life, realize and admit that life is frenetic and that you have anger issues, you have come to the right place. If, as a modern human being, you are experiencing all the problems associated with trying to survive in a world gone mad, then you are ready to take the first steps in finding the solutions you need. It is possible to survive and thrive in our modern world. All you need is the right foundation and the proper tools.

Who should be reading this book?

This book is for everyone who wants to live the best life possible. They seek a smooth ebb and flow, without the constant emotional upheavals that make them feel powerless and out of control.

It is for everyone who has felt like throwing their computer out the window, had a meltdown and screamed at their child who refused to listen, or felt like choking the inconsiderate driver who just cut them off. It is for anyone who felt their stomach churn with anxiety and stress over finances, exams, relationships or facing an unpleasant person in their work environment.

This book is for ordinary human beings who face a range of emotions every single day of their lives. It is for everyone tired of being ruled by out-of-control emotions that drain them, leaving little energy for anything productive. For every person who wants more out of life, who feels they are entitled to an enjoyable and fulfilling life.

Why is this important?

Look around you at the world we live in. Now imagine for a moment that you suddenly put a person from a long-gone age into our world and expect that person to function normally and be happy. It simply will not happen. That person's mind would not be able to cope. In his world, the 24-hour circadian clock determined when to wake up and when to sleep. Yet we are expected to cope daily in a world that is rapidly changing. We are taxed physically and emotionally to the utmost every day and expected to excel at everything.

Humans have not evolved to keep up with these changes. Our bodies have failed us. We are still coded with the flight or fight response that our ancestors in a more primitive world needed to survive. We cannot go back to live a simpler life in a slow-moving world. Therefore, we have to find solutions that will allow us to live well, without the stress, anger, and anxiety of daily life negatively affecting us.

CHAPTER ONE

ARE YOU REALLY IN CONTROL?

How did it come to this? Being emotionally out of control does not happen overnight. Getting to the point where you are now, desperately trying to hold everything together, was a journey. This happened due to a complex combination of factors. Yet it is not impossible to re-evaluate your life and set yourself on a new path based on a foundation of healthy emotional intelligence.

Different manifestations of anger

There are three basic ways we show anger. This does not mean that you express all of your anger in only one way. Situations that trigger your anger are diverse, and your reactions can vary depending on the circumstances. Some people may also have the tendency to favor a particular type of anger more than others.

External displays of anger

External anger is the most obvious, not only for the person your anger is directed at but also for everyone around you. Projecting your anger outwards can fluctuate from mild to extremely severe reactions and is a good indication of exactly how out of control your anger issues have become.

When you thump your coffee cup down on the table, it is considered a mild outward show of anger. Slamming doors as you leave a room also falls into this category. People will look at you with a frown and think to themselves that your anger is getting a tad out of control. They probably feel you are acting rather childish, but most will shrug this off and move on with their day.

Screaming abuse at drivers on the road that irritate you, whether your irritation is justified or not, is no longer considered a mild show of anger. Road rage can escalate and turn ugly very fast if you have been under severe stress for a prolonged period of time. When your emotions are so far out of control that your angry outbursts fall into the category of public disturbances, the consequences can be devastating. You can lose your job, your personal relationships may break down, and this could even be the final straw for your spouse.

When your external displays of emotion spiral out of control, you need to immediately address your anger issues. Verbally or physically abusing people, feeling that you are unable to walk away when another person shows confronts you, or retaliating violently means that your emotions have reached the critical out of control stage. When this happens, you have already caused incredible damage to all areas of your life.

Internal, self-directed anger

Thoughts directed at yourself (self-talk) can and should be a healthy way of boosting yourself emotionally. When anger and negative emotions are brought into the equation, the result is the exact opposite. Constantly telling yourself that you are stupid, ugly, too fat, or worthless will cause you to start hating yourself.

When you direct enough negativity and anger inwards, it leads to depression. You no longer want to do things that you have always enjoyed. Self-denial through anger ranges from isolating yourself from people at home or work and withdrawing socially to extreme cases where you may punish yourself by not eating.

Passive-aggressive anger

Displays of passive-aggressive anger are tricky and not as clearly defined as displays of outward anger and self-directed anger. People around you do not always realize that the sarcastic comments and negativity in your tone are driven by anger. Often people think you are just a mean-spirited person who indulges in bouts of juvenile sulking. The hardest part of passive-aggressive anger is that you yourself may not be fully aware that your actions and behavior are signs of anger.

You also show passive anger through deep apathy, doing poorly at work or school, and dysfunctional social behavior. (Santos-Longhurst, 2019).

Is anger a problem in your life?

Doctors and therapists very often hear their patients say that their anger is just a part of life, as everyone feels strong emotions from time to time. It is easy for people to justify their inability to manage their anger as infrequent incidents of extreme irritation in their very busy lives.

When your anger flares up frequently and for prolonged periods, it is a problem and can no longer be rationalized as simply extreme annoyance or irritability. Getting aggressive when the slightest thing goes wrong and losing your temper over minor incidents clearly show that you have a problem and need to find strategies to control your emotions in the long term.

You have a problem with anger when it negatively affects your relationship with your loved ones. In fact, your uncontrolled anger will have a major impact on all the different types of relationships you have in your life, including your work environment and your career.
When anger causes emotional distress to others, and your actions hurt the feelings of those it is directed at,

then you know it is a problem.

Being physically, emotionally and verbally abusive under any circumstances indicates a problem and no amount of generalization can classify your anger issues as annoyance or irritation. There is no need to be despondent, as there are numerous anger management strategies and solutions available. These will give you the power to turn your emotions around and take control

Lack of emotional intelligence in your life

When you are emotionally out of control and lack the emotional intelligence to deal with your anger, you create a ripple effect that circles outwards and negatively impacts each and every facet of your life.

Therefore, to deal with your anger issues you need to look at the bigger picture that is your life and understand how far-reaching the effects of it really are (Bradberry & Greaves, 2005).

Family and friends

Your significant other becomes quieter as time goes on, too hesitant to discuss issues with you. In fact, your partner will stop asking for any input from you, even regarding everyday events, for they simply never know what will trigger your angry tirade. You may even become angry enough to lash out physically at members of your family.

Your friends will start fading from your life. No matter how much they like you and care about you, once they realize you no longer bring value to their lives, they will start leaving. Friends are hugely important in every person's life, but when your out of control emotions start to distress them and make them feel embarrassed or fearful of your next outburst, they will look to their own best interests. Friends cannot be treated as your whipping boys for your own emotional issues. This creates a vicious circle of increased stress and anxiety that leads to even more anger inside you.

Work and colleagues

When you are unable to self-regulate your anger at work, your job and income becomes threatened. A smoothly running and productive workplace is only possible when people are happy to come to work. When you bring your uncontrolled emotions into the workspace, it affects not only your own productivity, but every person who encounters you during your workday.

The chain of command will soon notice the drop in productivity, which is a red flag for your continued employment at that company. Nobody is indispensable. You can and will be replaced by someone who has learned to use self-discipline techniques to deal with the many difficulties of any workplace.

Think for a moment about the fact that each of your colleagues have their own issues to deal with. They all have their own lives and the pressure, stress, and anxiety that are part of these daily routines. They truly do not want to, and definitely should not have to deal with whatever issues are going on in your personal life. They will become unresponsive to you, and stop offering help and advice. This will lead to you becoming very isolated and detached from everyone you work with.

Social interaction

Social interaction is a minefield for anyone with anger issues. You are prone to misunderstanding what others mean, as you are always on edge at social gatherings. Being on edge automatically pushes up your anxiety and stress levels. This too often leads to you to draw the wrong conclusions in a situation. This, in turn, can cause a show of aggression, and you fall back into the negative and destructive patterns of behavior that you have always used.

People will not stay around a person that they do not feel comfortable with during any type of social interaction. Depending on the type of social gathering, this once again will impact your work, family, and activities, or in other words, essentially every aspect of your life.

Cultivating empathy, a key aspect of emotional intelligence, both with yourself and with others, will completely change how you experience social interaction.

Anger and Aggression

First of all, you need to understand that anger and aggression are not the same thing. Anger can be healthy, and as a human being with emotions, you will experience anger from time to time. How you channel that anger is what makes it either a healthy emotion or an emotion that becomes negative and destructive. When the lines blur between being only mildly irritated and having an extreme outburst of anger, it is time to admit to yourself that you need anger management.

When anger, a normal human emotion, immediately leads to a display of aggression, you are heading for trouble.

When you lash out at the airline employee because your plane is delayed, you start a ripple effect. She will be upset and humiliated and you might end up in the worst possible seat. Your frustration and stress escalate, your blood pressure goes up, and when you step off that plane you are going to snap at everyone you come into contact with, completely needlessly.

The instinctive fight response

Physical signs of the flight response

- Your heart rate rapidly increases, putting unnecessary strain on your heart.
- Your hands and often your whole body start shaking, leading to anxiety and fear that people may notice this.
- Your stomach feels as if it is tied up in knots, often accompanied by nausea.
- Excessive sweating, which is very noticeable to the people around you.
- Your breathing becomes very shallow, making you lightheaded and in some cases can bring on a severe dizzy spell.
- Your mind starts racing, making it very difficult to concentrate and form coherent thoughts.
- Your muscles tense up, especially in the shoulders and neck and for many people an immediate headache follows.

As the primordial human reaction, the instinctive 'fight' response is part of human nature. This immediate, overwhelming fight response is what often stood between survival and extinction for your ancestors. This was essential in their world, but society has radically changed. So why are we still reacting in this way?

The oldest part of our brain is the amygdala, which is responsible for our emotions. So, when we perceive that we are threatened through fear and anxiety, the amygdala can bypass the newer part of our brain, the cortex which is the reasoning and thinking part.

When this happens, it is called an *amygdala hijack* (Goleman, 1996). The brain starts a chain reaction that overrides rational thinking, and you go into the flight, freeze or fight mode. This leads to irrational reactions and destructive behavior.

Our bodies have not evolved and changed at the same speed as our world has changed. To bring our emotions into alignment with the demands of our modern world we need to alter our behavior patterns so that our fight response is not triggered, giving us the ability to resolve conflict situations in a positive way.

Responsibility for your actions

When you get so angry that you have an irrational emotional outburst, it is not really about what is happening at that specific moment. When you lose control after your spouse threatens to leave you, is not about the words spoken, but about feeling inadequate and helpless to stop the hurt you feel inside. When you scream abuse at the driver who cut you off when you were running late for work, it's not about that action, but about how you feel disrespected and worthless.

These emotions were inside you for some reason, whether it is frustration over things happening at work or old memories of being bullied at school. So, when the guy at the intersection cuts you off, that triggers all these hidden emotions and causes you to react violently.

If you want to change your intense reaction to situations, you must be totally honest with yourself. Stop blaming others or events out of your control. Realize you cannot control the behavior of other people, but it is within your power to change your own destructive patterns of anger, and create balance in your own life.

CHAPTER TWO

HOW ANGER RUINS YOUR LIFE

N obody wants to accept that chronic anger ruins their lives physically, as well as their mental well-being. It is an uncomfortable truth to come to grips with. Sadly, that is exactly what happens to anyone who has chronic anger issues.

The body and the brain are complex biological machines that can only function optimally for so long when subjected to ongoing anger issues. The body will start to falter and this opens up the door for illness. In the same way, this happens with the brain, and the quality of your well-being starts deteriorating.

Your health

Your immune system is the defense that guards your health at all times. Once anger starts to have an impact on your immune system, this leaves your body vulnerable, not only to a multitude of infections and toxins but it also makes your body much more prone to chronic illnesses.

Prolonged anger plays havoc with your blood pressure and this, in turn, starts affecting your heart rate. The consequence of being angry all the time is an increased risk of coronary illnesses and heart attacks (Schroeder, 2017).

Undisciplined anger also significantly heightens the risk of stroke by up to three times, compared to a person who self-regulates their emotional responses. The risk factor increases when the person with anger issues already has a dormant aneurism they probably do not even know about.

When you are always irritable and angry, you become accident-prone, as the anger makes you less focused on whatever task you are doing, and this is a dangerous combination for anyone handling sharp objects or machinery.

As if this is not alarming enough, the increased health risks will also mean significant and unnecessary health care expenses. This, in turn, brings on more stress and anxiety that has a negative impact on your mental well-being.

Your mental well-being

When you carry anger around inside you without finding positive outlets, and never learn self-discipline techniques, your mental well-being suffers greatly. Anxiety and stress are not the only issues you then have to deal with. Chronic anger exhausts you both physically and mentally. You are always tired, yet you cannot sleep, as your mind is too busy brooding. So now you can add insomnia to the list of problems you have to deal with, and a tired mind leaves you unable to think clearly and be productive at work. All these factors turn you into a moody person who is no fun to be around at work, at home or at social gatherings.

Anxiety and Stress

Anxiety and stress have become such a normal part of life for so many modern humans, that we have become quite blasé about it. We pull our shoulders back and ask the doctor for a prescription to fix the problem. We then go right back to our old, well-established behavior patterns, never really thinking about what we are doing to ourselves. Then we are surprised and blame the doctor and the medication for not doing its jobs and being the quick fix, we expected. The downward spiral becomes more and more severe, when all you really have to do is learn the techniques to manage and control your anger.

Depression

Clinical studies show a definite link between uncontrolled anger and depression. Once you have reached this point, it is time to take stock, re-evaluate your quality of life, and start on a new journey to break free permanently from anger, stress, and anxiety to live the full, rich life you deserve.

Personal relationships

Your relationships suffer greatly from anger, as family and friends no longer trust you and people become uncomfortable around you. They will start closing off emotionally around you for fear that something they say or do will be a trigger and you will erupt in anger. You can cause emotional scarring that will stay with them for life by your uncontrolled anger, especially when children witness your outbursts.

Workplace relationships

In any company where you have people with a multitude of views and experiences, you will find that there will always be a difference of opinions when tasks, work methods or other management skills are discussed, and often the discussions can become quite passionate.

We all have to function within a bigger organization if we want to have a career. How you handle these debates and disputes makes the difference between being in a happy, vibrant workplace or be in a toxic one.

When you cannot control your emotions and diffuse your anger, and instead lash out at everyone, the whole atmosphere becomes negative. You become isolated as work colleagues move away from the toxic environment you have created. If you work in a client-oriented job, your anger and aggression is the surest way to lose clients and revenue.

Your career is on the line

Workplaces and careers have changed radically as the world becomes faster. The pace of life has escalated tremendously since technology and the internet revolutionized how, when and where we can pursue our careers.

Add to that the fact that economies worldwide are extremely tight and it is a dog eat dog world to earn a sustainable income, and it is only natural for tensions around the workplace to run high. People scramble for jobs and will often take on ones far below realistic market value, simply to know that they will have a paycheck at the end of the month. The result is that existing in the workplace is like walking a tightrope for many people.

None of this is good news for anyone who is battling

with their emotions. The reality is that countless jobs have been lost because of a lack of anger management and numerous careers have been sunk as spectacularly as the Titanic.

Sinking your career is absolutely not an option, especially when you have all the strategies and tools at hand to learn to control your anger. Even if you have all the right in the world to be angry at a specific person or incident in the workplace, you can control how you react to the situation.

An outburst of anger stops any chance of rational communication between parties. Once negative emotions come into play, you have lost the battle and the meeting effectively ends right there. Even if others attending try and salvage it, nothing constructive will emerge, as everyone is on edge.

Be aware of your feelings, and never ignore the signals your body and mind are giving you. Implement one or more of your coping mechanisms; Removing yourself from the room under the pretext of needing the bathroom is always acceptable. If leaving the room is not an option, take a few moments to refocus your mind and use a personal mantra to take your feelings of stress and anger down a few notches.

Workplace confrontations will happen, it's simply inevitable. How you handle those confrontations though will make the difference between your continued employment or, if you give in to explosive temper, your termination.

Taking responsibility and admitting to the other party that you need to take time out is crucial. It is not a sign of weakness, but instead shows maturity and strength on your part, as you are admitting you do not want to have the confrontation escalate. Smile and explain to the other person that you want to come back and continue the discussion without heated emotions. The confrontation will successfully de-escalate, no one's feelings will be hurt, and you can continue your day with no animosity and no extra stress.

Assertiveness versus aggression

It is not always possible to have time to cool down at work and get your anger under control. You have to deal with whatever is happening right at the moment.
In these types of situations, the outcome of the incident will be determined by several factors. Ultimately, it comes down to the difference between being assertive or being aggressive. This is especially important for women. It isn't fair that women are judged differently for behavior that is seen as acceptable for men, but this is the reality of our imperfect world.

Focus on using words that are assertive and do not come across as aggressive. Saying things such as "you messed up when you did this" will immediately be seen as aggressive. Instead, turn the situation around by making it about how you feel, not about what the other person did. Admitting to being stressed and frustrated about an incident does not diminish you as a person, but it makes people see you as an approachable human being.

Your body language and mannerisms are the most important factor in how you present yourself and can clearly convey either assertiveness or aggression. Speaking calmly with a smile and using rational statements will not hurt the feelings of the other party. Instead, it makes them feel more at ease and they will not feel that they are being attacked. Aggressive behavior on your part will trigger the other person's fight mode, as they will feel insulted, not valued, and like you are trying to intimidate them.

Practice turning a situation around from potentially career-damaging to a calm and rational discussion. By preparing for assertiveness versus aggression in front of a mirror, you will be ready when a situation arises. Closely observe your facial expressions and body language. This is an exercise in self-awareness and anger management that you need to learn and implement in workplace conflicts as soon as possible.

Own your anger and stop deflecting blame

We all use the same time-worn clichés to explain why

it is everyone else's fault except our own that we have anger issues, because our emotions are uncontrolled. This is how we try and convince ourselves that the world is not fair, that people are out to make our lives miserable.

You may try to justify to yourself and everyone else around you why you lost your temper. It is easy to come up with a never-ending list. Your father was hot-tempered, so it is normal for you to be the same way. The other driver is at fault or your business partner does not know how to run the company. At home, your spouse is argumentative when she knows she should keep quiet and the children never do the tasks you want them to do. You had too much to drink, so it's not your fault you got into a brawl at the pub. Your buddies should have stopped you from drinking so much.

The roots of our problems with anger can be traced back to our early years. Looking back on your life, there are many reasons why you never developed healthy outlets for anger.

Parents are not always the best role models. You may have grown up in a home where incessant arguments were normalized by parents who also had anger issues or were not emotionally capable of the responsibilities of being parents.

We all have a good laugh at the memes people create shaming their pets for bad behavior and send them on to all our friends on social media. What the memes portray is what many people experienced in their lives after they were caught doing something wrong and admitted to it. People carry the memories of being harshly disciplined and often shamed in front of family members when they honestly admitted that they were at fault. For anyone who experienced this, their defense tactic became shifting blame onto anyone and anything else. As adults, we continue these habits formed in our early years, regardless of the effect it has on our lives and relationships.

Many people grow up with a deep need to make themselves appear better than they really are. They believe that having no imperfections and shifting blame is how they validate their own actions.

We all have stories to tell and experiences we had that negatively influenced our ability to deal with our emotions. The consequence of blame-shifting, no matter what happened in the past, is that you are the one left with anger issues that you refuse to acknowledge.

Shifting blame becomes a destructive strategy to avoid having to take an honest look at yourself. You can continue to push off the painful self-examination that is needed to take responsibility for your anger and aggression for years. This will only result in impulsive actions with negative results.

Be kind to yourself. You are human and every human

on the planet has faults, weaknesses, and shortcomings. It is only once you stop blaming others and take full responsibility for how you handle your anger that you can learn, with the help of coping strategies, to handle situations of stress and anger in a positive manner (Golden, 2018).

CHAPTER THREE

TIME TO TAKE STOCK

O nce you have acknowledged that your emotions are out of control, it is time to take stock of how your anger issues have impacted on the various areas of your life. This is essential to prevent all aspects of your life from falling apart like a row of dominoes.

After you have completed an honest review of your life, it is time to get serious about anger management and emotional intelligence. For you to succeed in your goal of managing your anger, you need to understand the five elements of emotional intelligence and how you can use these elements to take your life from out of control to self-disciplined. It is through using these techniques that you will finally be able to bring balance back into your life.

People most often consider emotional intelligence as it is applied to the workplace, and often speak of the importance of emotional intelligence for leaders. It is useful here, but it is just as important for every person who has to survive and cope with all the complex interactions of home and family, relationships, work, and life on a daily basis.

The five foundation stones of emotional intelligence

- Self-awareness
- Self-management/self-regulation
- Social skills and developing relationships
- Motivating yourself
- Empathy

It is very important to differentiate between intelligence quotient and emotional intelligence. Someone with a genius-level IQ can have the worst possible EQ skills, while someone with an average IQ could have top-notch EQ skills and far more successfully manage whatever emotional issues they might have.

You first need to understand *why* you have problems dealing with anger before you can start on a new path of learning to manage your anger and prevent your emotions from taking over. Your brain is incredibly powerful, but because we still have the fight or flight instinct, the emotional part and the reasoning part clash. Instinctively, the emotional side wants to take over, as a way to ensure survival. The result is often outbursts of anger and aggression, as the reasoning part of your brain backs down and lets the emotions rule.

Fortunately for all of us, with the right tools and strategies, it is possible to change this. We can learn through EQ strategies to stop this instinctive and irrational emotional hijacking from taking place. Far too often we hear that we are simple creatures and slaves to our emotions. That is not true at all. If we were true, we would not have the reasoning part of our brain, as it would be useless. We have the choice to stay emotional slaves, or we can use EQ to manage our anger. It is not difficult to do, all it takes is honesty and practice (Bradberry & Greaves, 2009).

So, what does this mean for you in your own life? How do you use these five elements to improve the quality of your life by bringing down your stress and anxiety levels?
The strategies work when you move past simply knowing what emotional intelligence means and start

applying the knowledge that you have gained. Knowing is simply not enough without the practical application. In the beginning, it might feel very overwhelming when you are in a very stressful situation or you are extremely anxious. This means you must practice and continue applying the self-regulation techniques until they become part of you. The goal you are working towards is worth every bit of effort you put into it.

Become self-aware

Self-managing your anger and stress is your goal. To be able to do that, you need to be able to make practical decisions that are both constructive and positive. So, you must first become self-aware and learn to recognize what you are really feeling. When you get angry, what core emotions are driving you to anger? Not all of us are fortunate enough to only carry positive emotional experiences from our childhood into adulthood. The emotional baggage, which we have never dealt with, is a huge obstacle for developing a healthy self-awareness. We cannot function without being aware. Until we connect to the emotions within us, it is impossible to become self-disciplined.

So, it is time to put your thinking cap on and figure out exactly where each of the emotions you feel at any specific time really come from. Remember, your emotions are your physical and mental reactions to something specific. It could be an event or a feeling, but it originates from a specific experience. In a nutshell, you must learn what makes you tick emotionally.

Becoming self-aware also means that you need to observe how your emotions affect the people around you. This is not a comfortable experience. It is far easier to simply try and ignore the fact that your emotions have a huge impact on every person you come into contact with.

Part of the process of becoming more self-aware is mindfulness. In our overly busy lives, we have fallen into the habit of not focusing fully on what is happening right here and right now. We drive to the shop while listening to the weather forecast and thinking ahead about what you must pack if it rains. Mothers do this all the time without even realizing it. They may be keeping an eye on the children while they are making dinner and doing laundry, while also watching what is happening on television. We are so busy multi-tasking that we never focus on our feelings and miss seeing so many positive and uplifting things happening around us.

By practicing mindfulness, you train your mind to focus directly on what is happening at the moment. We all gain something from this practice. When you engage in mindfulness, it makes you far more self-aware while decreasing your stress and anxiety levels.

As your self-awareness grows, you will better understand your own strengths and weaknesses. Becoming self-aware allows you to look logically at your strengths and weaknesses and find ways to use both of them to achieve a positive outcome. Be kind to yourself and stop hating your weaknesses. Accept them as simply another part of what makes you who you are.

Self-discipline / self-management

To achieve self-discipline, you must first grow in self-awareness. You cannot self-manage your anger issues if you are not aware of what emotions cause certain reactions within yourself. These two elements of emotional intelligence go hand in hand.

So, what is self-management all about? It is the ability to manage how you react to situations through self-awareness of your emotions. It is the ability to act, or not act, when something happens. You can do this because self-awareness gives you the flexibility to 'think out of the box,' instead of immediately triggering the fight response.

Self-discipline is not only about stopping yourself from blowing up in a fiery rage. It is a lifelong commitment to yourself to understand and accept that you have anger issues. Accept it, but remember that you have the ability to change your reactions and find positive solutions to the triggers that made you react with anger and aggression in the past.

It is a long-term commitment, but it is neither difficult nor impossible. By using all the strategies and abundant physical and mental coping mechanisms available, it will soon become a normal part of your daily life. Every step you take along this journey will bring more and more benefits, as not only you change, but the people you interact with change as well.

Empathy and relationship building

Empathy starts with you. Stop getting angry when you do something wrong. Instead, start treating yourself with kindness. Forgive yourself for mistakes. Accept that you made an error, whether big or small, and move on from there. Find a positive solution to and implement it to avoid making the same mistake again in the future. You will not be able to treat other people with empathy until you start treating yourself with empathy. It is one of the most powerful weapons in your battle against anger.

Empathy and building strong, positive relationships go hand in hand. Your self-awareness allows you to become conscious of the feelings of other people and how they react to any given situation. This enables you to 'walk a mile in their shoes,' and makes you more flexible in how you deal with them. Having empathy towards other people opens your mind to their needs and wants and, most importantly, allows you to listen to what they have to say without an immediate emotional response.

When you are in any conflict-filled situation, being flexible and having empathy towards the other parties radically changes the outcome of that conflict. This, in turn, leads to better and stronger relationships on both sides, as you will understand them better. With time and practice, you will be able to build a positive relationship even with people that you do not really like.

Empathy and strong relationships change your family and workplace environment, as well as your social interactions. The stronger your relationships are, the bigger the change you will see in your own emotional reactions.

Self-motivation

To achieve your goal of managing your anger, you have to apply self-motivation. You need to bring the two parts of motivation, intrinsic and extrinsic, together to be successful. This will require you to combine what you want to achieve, and what you need to achieve. You want to balance your mental wellbeing and quality of life and you need to salvage your personal, work and social relationships.

When you combine both parts of motivation you have the perfect self-motivation formula that brings you internal as well as external benefits.
Self-motivation is a personal challenge. At the same time, self-motivation brings the external benefits of being accepted into social circles, better work relationships with possible promotions, and stronger bonds with family and friends.

As you apply self-motivation to achieving your goal

of anger management, your commitment will grow, which in turn fosters an even stronger drive to commit to your goal. Commitment sparks initiative to find more strategies that work for you and implement them in your life.

Once you have committed to self-motivation, you create a looping effect. You commit, achievement follows, encouraging more commitment. This cycle brings optimism to your life and lessens your stress and anxiety about successfully managing your anger. Commitment to self-motivation will affect every part of your life. It will bring about the changes you need to balance your life and shake off the shackles of your uncontrolled emotions.

Social awareness and interactions

Why are social awareness and the ability to interact with people so important for anyone with anger issues? When your emotions are out of control, it creates problems with social interactions, as people are unsure of how you will respond, especially in any stressful situation. This makes you unapproachable and can be a huge problem, particularly in the workplace.

Part of your anger management is to develop social awareness and build bonds that will encourage people to see you as a trustworthy person. Social awareness includes watching body language and facial expressions and allowing them to guide you towards better communication skills and more positive social interaction.

With heightened social awareness you will easily pick up the emotions of others and understand how they really feel. This enables you to handle situations with empathy instead of allowing your own emotions to dictate your actions. Self-awareness is looking inward and learning to understand who and what you are, whereas social awareness forces you to look outwards and learn about the people you interact with and help you understand their needs and desires.

All of these changes work together to enable you to handle conflict-filled situations calmly. Both self and social-awareness help prevent the thalamus from bypassing the cortex and sending signals directly to the amygdala. The is then able to make use of coping mechanisms that you have set in place. A stressful situation can then have a positive outcome.

One of the best training exercises you can do to develop your social awareness is to take regular time out to go people-watching. Simply sit quietly and observe people and see how they behave under different circumstances and situations. It will be time well spent and you will gain invaluable insights to enhance your own social awareness.

Social awareness techniques can be applied with equal

success in the workplace and in the family when it comes to better handling of conflict situations ("Understanding and Developing", 2016).

CHAPTER FOUR

SELF-CONTROL TO MANAGE ANGER

S elf-control, self-regulation, self-discipline, self-management. What they all boil down to is the ability to control your emotions in stressful situations. Yet for so many people this feels like a mountain too high to climb. They anticipate failure even before taking that first step to achieving self-control. However, with the right strategies in place and the willingness to learn, implementing self-control measures is within everyone's grasp.

Anger is a completely normal emotion that all

humans are capable of exhibiting. Uncontrolled anger, on the other hand, results in severe outbursts and aggressive behavior. It is usually completely disproportionate to the situation and can even lead to physical violence.

Too many people do not realize that controlling anger and suppressing anger are not the same thing. Suppression leads to a volcano of emotions brewing below the surface, whereas self-control anger can be channeled in a healthy way.

Debunking myths

There are several myths about anger. We hold onto these when we justify why we cannot control our emotions and our tempers. This is a great avoidance strategy to put our heads in the sand: we can't see the problem, so there is no problem. These myths allow us to pretend that things are not really as bad as they seem. We tell ourselves that we just need a holiday or we just need people just need to stop being so annoying and then everything will be just fine.

It's time to scrap that thinking and erase those myths. Deep down, that little voice of reason and honesty insists on telling you this is all an excuse. It is time to debunk these myths and get control over your anger issues.

The venting myth

Stop telling yourself that it is healthy to give in to anger, and that having a good venting session is better than trying to control your emotions and holding it all in. Anger is not an overinflated car tire that needs to release air in order to prevent damage. Instead, having temper tantrums can be compared to a volcano blowing, with streams of lava devastating everything in its path. You end up with more anger-related problems instead of lessening your anger, anxiety, and stress.

I just can't help getting angry

Claiming that it simply is not possible to control anger, it's an emotion and as such, there is absolutely nothing you can do about it, is nonsense. In order to justify this myth, people often add that their whole family is made up of hotheads, and you can't fight your genetics.

Please stop fooling yourself. You are parroting this myth to avoid acknowledging that you have anger issues that you need to learn to manage.

You cannot control or even change the situation that triggers your anger, as you do not have control over other people, and you cannot change the weather that may cause you to miss a very important meeting. Of course, you will feel angry and frustrated. These are normal human emotions. How you react to these emotions at that specific time, however, is something you that you do have control over. You have the choice to lose your temper and become aggressive, both verbally and physically, or to deal with your emotions through anger management.

Aggression earns respect

This is the top myth people with anger problems bring into the workplace. If you insist that getting angry and aggressive earns you respect, and believe this is that the fastest way to get things done, you are only deceiving yourself.

People do not jump to do what you want because they think you are a great leader and respect you. They do it because they are scared. They are trying to avoid becoming a casualty of your erupting temper. If you want people to respect you, you have to earn it. Treat them with dignity and they will listen to you. If you put in the extra effort, they will do as you request with a smile and respect you for being a decent person (Segal and Smith, 2019).

What are you really feeling?

Learn to identify what emotions are really behind your anger in any given situation. Are you anxious about changes at work, stressed about an upcoming exam or worried about unexpected expenses? An honest examination of your feelings is needed before you impulsively react with emotion instead of rational thinking.

Take note of physical warning signs

People often say that there are no warning signs before their outbursts of anger. This is not true. Before a rush of emotions, you need to start taking note of how you physically react. Your body actually is trying to warn you of the approaching storm, but often we simply ignore these signs. However, once you recognize these physical warning signs for what they are, you can take the necessary steps to lower your stress levels and avert an uncontrolled emotional outburst.

There are common warning alerts that everyone has, you just need to be aware of them to be able to put the brakes on in time.

Clenching and grinding your teeth

When you start grinding your teeth and tightening your jaw, or realize that you are clenching and unclenching your hands, your body is warning you that your emotions are rising.

Body starts accelerating

Your body starts accelerating in anticipation of anger. Your breathing becomes faster and shallower, and your heartbeat speeds up. Often this is accompanied by feeling flushed or sweaty. Your body is warning you that it is about to go into the fight or flight mode.

Pacing

Restlessness is one of the easiest warning signs to identify. You find that you simply cannot sit still and need to keep moving, so you start pacing up and down. Often while pacing your stomach literally feels like it is being tied in knots. This takes things to the next level as your endless pacing winds you up faster to the point of explosion.

Muscle tension

Your shoulder muscles are the target of tension as your anger starts to build up. The closer you get to the boiling point, the worse the muscle ache in your shoulders becomes.

Headaches and inability to concentrate

People often complain of feeling foggy, not being able to concentrate, and a nagging headache that won't go away. Your body is trying very hard to send you warning signals that you should not ignore (Segal and Smith, 2019).

Learn to recognize what triggers you

To be able to use self-control to manage your anger, you need to first be able to identify what exactly acts as a trigger that pushes you over the edge. It is very important to know these signs, so if you need to, carry a notebook to document your triggers as they happen. The more information you have, the better prepared you will be to manage them.

By identifying your triggers, you will able to see patterns that point to unresolved issues that you may have buried deep in your subconscious mind. In order to move forward with self-control, you need to first take care of these underlying issues. Once the issue is resolved, whether it is anxiety or fear, or even feelings of guilt about something that happened a long time ago, these triggers will be far less powerful.

Be aware of what circumstances trigger you

Identify the circumstances that trigger your anger. For each person this is different. For many people, being overtired is a clear trigger. Exhaustion makes you irritable and you may be triggered by things that would not normally annoy you when you are well-rested. Anxiety and stress over deadlines or fear over a relationship issue that has been unresolved for too long also act as triggers. Once you identify the circumstances that cause your anger to be triggered, you can use self-control to stop you from doing and saying the wrong things. You will be able to turn impulsive choices into positive outcomes.

Categorize your triggers

Start keeping a trigger check sheet to track the different types you encounter. This is not a singular exercise. This is an ongoing task, and you will add information as you recognize more triggers. Have columns for the different types of triggers as well as possible solutions.

Ideally, you should try and avoid situations that trigger you, but this is not always possible, even when you make changes to your routine, your way of life, your work environment, and personal relationships.

Your trigger check sheet should also include a column where you detail strategies and solutions for triggers that you cannot avoid.

Not all emotions have the same triggers

Keep track of each emotional state that triggers you and how you can cope with that feeling.

Circumstances and activities triggers

A trigger can literally be anything, and it is important to keep notes so that you can see patterns emerge. You will then be able to avoid activities and situations that are triggering.

Negative thought triggers

When your mind dwells on negative thoughts, it is

not easy to recognize that this will trigger an unwanted anger response. Adding these thought triggers to your tracker sheet will make you so much more aware of them, and you can then set strategies and coping mechanisms in place to distract you from dwelling and pull you back before you respond emotionally.

People: Individuals or Groups

It is simply not possible to like every single person you interact with. Some will irritate you more than others, and some will immediately trigger your fight response. Avoid these people and groups of people if at all possible, as you simply do not need this type of stress in your life if you can steer clear of them. Unfortunately, there are times when you will need to interact with these people. This is where your tracker sheet becomes invaluable. It is impossible to find solutions and strategies to cope when you are already in the situation, so by keeping your tracker sheet on hand, you will be well prepared to interact with them. It is very important to practice scenarios and add coping mechanisms to your sheet so that you are prepared when you meet these people face to face. The people in your support system can be of great help in situations like these.

Places that trigger an emotional response

You may associate certain places with negative events or memories. Again, it is best to avoid these places, even if it means changing your routine. If you cannot avoid these trigger places, you have to find strategies to help you cope with your heightened emotions ("Triggers", 2017).

Choose to cultivate a new mindset

For you to successfully implement the necessary strategies of self-control, you must change how you think and develop a new mindset. You can no longer continue in the mindset you had, as this has brought you to this place where your uncontrolled emotions are ruining your life.

Your goal is to change from accepting your life as it is now and thinking that there is nothing you can do to change who you are, to understanding your new way of being. It is your choice to say to yourself and the whole world that you are choosing to be a person who has self-control over your emotions and is no longer ruled by impulsive, destructive behavior. Once you have chosen this new path, it is time to get to work.

Work means you are going to have to keep toiling to improve your self-control. It is not possible to overturn a lifetime of uncontrolled emotions in a day. You have a lot of work and practice ahead of you, but each time you implement a strategy and every time you are able to handle conflict without blowing up in anger, it is a huge achievement. This will encourage you to keep going, and one day you will suddenly realize that this self-controlled way of life has become a habit, and it is now an integral part of who you are (Schwantes, 2017).

Strategies

Humans have a morbid obsession with failure. We focus so intently on a mistake or a task we failed at that it totally overshadows the many achievements we have accomplished. We keep dwelling and brooding on our failures to the extent that they cause a great deal of stress and anxiety for us. Stop yourself in your tracks when you realize this is what you are doing, as this is a destructive behavior pattern that prevents you from moving forward. The more you dwell on failures, the harder it becomes for you to see that you are making progress.

With this in mind, you need to put some strategies in place that will immediately minimize the chances of failure. These strategies are not hidden secrets. We simply do not realize how much they can help us cope, and the far-reaching benefits that they hold for your life.

Food

Your body is a biological machine; it cannot survive without food. Food covers a broad spectrum though. It is all about what you put into your body that makes the difference.

Your body needs a constant, steady form of nutrition since your brain burns calories very fast when you engage in self-control to manage your anger. So, you need to feed your brain to be able to practice self-control.

When you grab a candy bar because you feel tired, the only thing you achieve is causing your sugar levels to shoot up, soon followed by your glucose levels crashing. So instead of feeding your brain the much-needed nutrition it craves, you become exhausted and feel totally drained. That candy bar is not evil. You simply need to learn when you should eat that and when you should take in another form of nutrition.

To prolong the time, you have to engage self-control before you have to eat again, go for foods that can be classified as slow-burning, complex carbohydrates. You do not need a sugar rush when you are about to go into an important meeting or start writing that final exam, as that only spells disaster.

Good examples of slow-burning foods to keep at hand include:

- Oatmeal and barley.
- Eggs, turkey and tuna.
- Cottage cheese and Greek yoghurt.
- Fruits such as apples and bananas.
- Vegetables high in complex carbs; green vegetables, sweet potatoes, potatoes, corn, and pumpkin.
- Wholegrain pasta and rice.
- Protein bars for emergencies.

Food is vitally important; make a list of slow-burning foods that you like best and eat those, especially when you know you are heading to a stressful event.

Contemplation and inner reflection

Inner reflection and contemplation are an essential part of your journey to control your emotions through anger management. No matter how busy your daily life is, you need to make time; make yourself and your wellbeing top priority.

It is not always possible to take long periods of time during your day. You can however take short time-out periods throughout the day. Even five-minute periods to walk away from everything and focus only on yourself will boost your ability to self-control.

Go and sit in a garden or find a place that makes you feel comfortable and stress-free. Tune out all external distractions and thoughts and turn your mind inward. Focus only on your senses and slow your breathing. For this short period, nothing else matters. Make this a daily habit and you will soon see a huge improvement in your self-awareness. This can help you block impulsive behavior that is both negative and destructive.

Move your body

This wonderful biological machine you have called your body comes with a built-in fail-safe, known as a neurotransmitter called GABA. It has the specific function of soothing your mind in a way that will help you focus on self-control. The trick with this neurotransmitter is that for it to activate, you actually have to move your body.

This means you have to get off your chair and stop brooding about whatever is stressing you out. This does not mean that you have to go run a marathon. You can do something as simple as walking. By the time you come back to the situation that was triggering you, your brain has done its job of soothing and you have resisted that impulsive behavior.

Impulse and temptation

Giving in to your impulses is so easy to do, and you then end up with stress and anger because of your failure. Temptation comes in many forms, and some are far easier to resist than others. Take note of which temptations in your life are the most difficult to resist, and make those are a priority to tackle. Get the temptations that feel like big rocks in your path down to pebbles by implementing the 10-minute rule.

The 10-minute resistance rule works like this: force yourself to wait out those 10 minutes before you give in to the impulse. By the end of that time, you will have shrunk that boulder down to a pebble that you can side-step with ease.

The more you practice this 10-minute rule, the better your impulse control becomes. So, what if you do not succeed every time? You are human and humans have ups and downs. Mark the experience as part of your learning on this journey to a balanced life free from the control of your emotions.

Be kind to yourself

Stop beating yourself up about having failures as you develop your self-control. Self-control takes time, practice and determination to succeed. Dwelling on your failures as you progress is harmful, leads to self-hatred, and takes you back down that old path of stress and anxiety that can easily lead to depression.

You will still feel bad about your failures. That is normal. But fixating on those failures breaks down all the effort you have put into learning self-control. When you feel you are slipping back into the routine of hating yourself for your failures, visualize a huge red flag in your mind. Red equals danger, and danger means stop and remove those thoughts from your mind. Instead of dwelling, start looking at solutions to prevent that failure in the future. This shift of focus from dwelling to solution finding removes that red flag and allows you to move forward.

Make this your catch-phrase: be kind to myself and treat myself with empathy and respect. Never forget that no matter how much effort you need to put in to reach your goal of self-control and managing your anger, you are worth it. With each new strategy you implement and coping mechanism you set in place; you are forming new healthy habits that replace the old, destructive habits. These habits will stay with you for the rest of your life, each one part of the foundation you build to keep your emotions under control and balanced (Bradberry & Greaves, 2005).

Rules of engagement for couples

Arguments, especially in personal relationships, will happen. How you handle the argument determines whether you damage the relationship or make it stronger. Anger and arguments within a romantic relationship are more delicate, as this is not a situation you want to walk away from.

Always fight fair

No name-calling or criticizing of your partner. Using

derogatory names and making demeaning statements only breaks down your partner. It is not fair to use emotional blackmail during an argument by threatening to leave. Even though you are angry, keep it clean.

Digging up old history

You must focus on this argument and the issues here and now. Dragging issues from the past into this argument is not fair and defeats any chance of finding a healthy solution to the present conflict.

Priorities

Relationships are not games where you keep score of how many quarrels you have won. Your most important priorities are your commitment, strengthening the bonds of love you share, and finding healthy solutions.

Agree to disagree

People come from different backgrounds and have different sets of values that they bring into a relationship. When this causes conflict, the only way to handle it is with empathy. Agree to disagree and call a truce, as the relationship is more important than getting your own way and trying to force your values and views onto your partner.

This rule applies not only to conflict due to different values but in any argument between you and your spouse. When you realize that the argument will not be resolved, choose to end it before your temper flares out of control.

Forgiveness

You cannot go into an argument with the view that you want to get even for any hurt you feel, or that your partner deserves to be punished. If you hope to resolve the argument in a positive way, you must learn to forgive your partner for anything said or done in the past.

Passive-aggressive avoidance

Using passive-aggressive avoidance tactics to evade dealing with the issue at hand will only prolong the argument, and this in turn will only bring more tension into the household and the relationship.

Back to school

Not everyone has pleasant memories of their school days, often with very good reason. So hearing they must go back to school does not sit well with them. That is exactly what you have to do, however, to reap the benefits of the choice you have made. In order to become a strong, self-aware human who is in control of your emotions and has kicked your anger issues to the curb, you must adopt a learning mindset.

Going back to school simply means taking advantage of every possible source of assistance available to you in order to make it easier to achieve your goals. The internet provides an abundance of resources and tools to jumpstart your learning.

Anger management worksheets, journal templates and checklists are freely available. Take some time and look around. When you take notes, you have a visual record, and it is a well-known fact that visual input makes a greater impact than mental notes alone.

CHAPTER FIVE

PRACTICAL COPING MECHANISMS

I n the 17th century, the English poet John Donne wrote the words, "No man is an island, entire of itself." Today, 400 years later, those words still hold true. No one can stand alone and in isolation. We all need each other, otherwise, our world becomes much smaller and we grow weaker.

No-one wants to live an isolated life, cut off from family, friends and work colleagues. Uncontrolled emotions isolate you and make you feel that you are invisible. The toll this takes on your relationships and your career can be devastating. The familiar vicious cycle of increased stress, anxiety, and depression leads to more anger and even less control over your emotions.

Choose to not live like this any longer and break down the walls of that self-imposed isolation with anger management. By using all the strategies and coping mechanisms available through developing and growing your emotional intelligence, you will find success.

Practical coping mechanisms are crucial to change how you react to anger, and with these in place, you will make changes to all aspects of your life. The great thing is that there is no shortage of coping mechanisms; some you may know and others you have not thought about. You need all the help you can get, so grab them, use them, and make them your own.

Separate healthy from unhealthy coping strategies

Everyone needs coping strategies in their lives to deal with whatever issues they might have. They give you the ability to better understand those uncontrolled emotions. The problem, though, is that we are impatient beings. We want everything to be fixed immediately. It is understandable, because our world is fast and everything happens instantaneously. We no longer have to write letters and send them off through snail mail. Instead, we call or use an app on our smartphones to instantly connect. It is the same with food. We grab fast food instead of cooking a healthy meal at home. For so many of us, the quick fix and instant gratification have become a normal way of life.

So, when it comes to implementing coping mechanisms to help us deal with anger and uncontrolled emotions, we automatically turn to any available quick fix. We just want to feel better, and we want to feel better right now.

Those unhealthy coping strategies bring fast, but temporary relief, soon to be followed by the crash of emotions. We then have extra stress and anger to deal with because we, in fact, did not solve anything at all.

What you need to do right from the start of anger management is to make a clear separation between healthy and unhealthy options.

Unhealthy quick fixes

We grab a drink to numb the emotional distress and some of us set off on the road of recreational drugs. Both works only temporarily, and when you are sober, the anger is still there, with added problems you now have to deal with.

Withdrawing socially is another way to try and cope and by doing this, your isolation and disconnection from life just gets worse. More stress and more anxiety kick in, until depression grips you and you stop caring about yourself. Your appearance, and your health, and well-being start to deteriorate, fast.

Food is another quick fix. We use it as a crutch that unbalances our emotional well-being and leads to more anger issues. You may start hating yourself and feel disgusted with what you perceive to be a weakness.

We use procrastination in the hope that somehow the task we cannot cope with or do not want to deal with at that time will miraculously vanish. In the workplace, this behavior is soon noticed and you will earn the reputation of an untrustworthy slacker.

When you take a rational look at the unhealthy quick fixes, we can clearly see the pattern of self-destruction. It becomes clear that all coping strategies are not equal, and it is worth it to investigate the long-term benefits of implementing healthy options. Patience is key when deciding on the best coping strategies and the benefits you reap from these slower strategies are greater.

Healthy, long-term coping options

Get your support system in place as soon as possible. This means involving everyone in your life. Open up and talk about having anger issues and that you choose to use anger management to turn your life around. Speak to your doctor and get valuable medical insights to help you along.

Social support is necessary and when people you socialize with are in the know, they can help you defuse volatile conditions in situations of stress.

Take stock of your nutritional needs specific to your daily diet and build a comprehensive list of healthy food choices with long term benefits. Again, you should include family, friends and your workplace support.

For the majority of people who have serious anger issues, it has taken a lifetime to get to this point and has involved affected everyone you know. Now it is time to involve each of them in your goal of achieving freedom from this anger.

There are many easy and practical coping strategies that work wonders to bring your anger under control. As you progress on your journey, you may find other methods that are relevant to you.

Zip your lips

Do not impulsively blurt out the first thing that pops into your head. Keep quiet and allow your brain to do its work so that you can rationally think. Control your breathing while you think. This immediately lessens the stress, and your mind will be much clearer.

Stopwatch actions

To stop yourself from impulsive actions that you will most likely regret, implement the stopwatch coping mechanism. Your wristwatch or your cell phone app will serve as a timer to prevent you from overreacting. Pick a time and stick to it. Five minutes can be an eternity when you feel your anger is about to explode. The more you practice this strategy, the easier and more effective it becomes.

Use count down

If the stopwatch strategy is not available or not appropriate for a situation, use a countdown. If possible, find a quiet place, or walk down a passage, or go to the bathroom. Mentally or even verbally count backward. Start from 100 and slowly count down, clearing your mind and regulating your breathing. This works very well to pull the fuse out of the timebomb of your anger.

Relaxation and exercise

It would be great if you could dash out of a stressful meeting and go to the gym to run your anger off on a treadmill or go lift weights to distress. However, this is definitely not going to be appropriate in the middle of work and most likely will get you fired. Thankfully there are many options available that won't get you fired or get you labeled as the office nutcase.

Simply walking will do the trick. Take a walk down a passage on the pretext that you need to go fetch files or a data printout. Whatever works best to remove you for a short period of time from the stressful situation and prevent an angry eruption.

Your muscles warn you loud and clear that you are building up to an uncontrolled emotional response. Unlock them systematically, starting with neck rotations and stretches, then rolling your shoulders until you feel the clenched muscles relax. Do muscle relaxation for every part of your body that is affected by the approaching bout of anger. Stretching exercises are another great way to unlock your muscles and distress fast. Use whatever combinations work best for you. You know your body best, so adapt these quick relaxation and exercise routines until you have a fast distressing routine that you can use in even the most stressful and volatile situations.

You are priority number one

How often have you used the phrases "I am too busy for this or that" and "I don't have the time in my schedule to relax"? Erase these two phrases immediately from your vocabulary. As of this moment, they no longer exist. If those phrases were of any value to you, you would not now be at a crossroads where your emotions have gotten totally out of control. Make a list of self-care activities, however small they may be, then implement them as part of your daily or weekly routine. Small things like taking a few minutes to catch up with world news, checking what new book your favorite author is working on, or watching a new movie are easy ways to prioritize your own well-being. Then make sure that your family and friends know that these times are yours and not to be interrupted. The world will not collapse into ruin if you are not answering the chat app for 10 minutes or do not immediately stop what you are doing to attend to their needs.

Make walking a daily routine

Yes, we are back to getting your body moving. Most of us live a very sedentary life, as we are stuck in an office staring at computer screens all day. Our bodies are designed for movement and need this in order to function properly. The excuse of not having access to a state-of-the-art gym, or not being a super athlete is not applicable. Whatever your environment is, or wherever you live, find a suitable place that you feel comfortable with and start walking. Walking must become a daily routine for you in order to get your body to start helping you towards your goal. You will be quite surprised by what you experience on your daily walks. You may see flowers and trees you hardly noticed before, or realize that the neighbor who you always thought of as a sour apple actually does smile. The benefits are far-reaching; it is literally a wake-up call to stop and smell the roses. Just going for a walk each day improves not only your physical health, but it is also a great mood enhancer and boosts your mental well-being.

Yoga

Yoga and meditation are two extremely powerful coping mechanisms in your anger management arsenal. The physical and mental well-being benefits of yoga and meditation are with you for life and can be used at work or at home, in all circumstances. The benefits of yoga are not only restricted to formal workouts. You can use the techniques to calm yourself no matter where you are.

Yoga classes take you past the basics of yoga to the advanced techniques and poses. These techniques and poses include many that are specifically designed to address anger issues and promote anger management. Classes also offer group support, which is an emotional benefit for you during your progress to bring your emotions under control.

Certain yoga breathing exercises focus on releasing anger, and once you have mastered these exercises you use them easily to bring down your stress levels (Griffin, 2019).

Meditation

Clinical studies show that meditation has both immediate and long-term benefits. These can assist in making your uncontrolled emotions manageable, and even people at the beginner stage of meditation feel the physical benefits from their first session. Making meditation a long-term solution for anger management helps your physical and mental well-being. Meditation teaches you to not have a volatile reaction to anger, and with practice, you will respond to anger in a positive way.

Take a moment and visualize your relationships, your work environment and your social interactions after you have started practicing meditation regularly. That image will be radically different from your life right now (Wei, 2016).

Quick destress by using your five senses

You have five senses, do not let them go to waste. Put them to good use as a practical coping mechanism. Most of us do not really think of using our senses to quickly drop our stress levels down a few notches. Instead, we just accept our senses as things that allow us to hear the phone ring, smell the food burning on the stove, or see the road ahead as we race off to work each morning.

Make a cup of tea or coffee and sit quietly and savor the aroma with each sip you take. Use your sense of touch to stroke a loved pet and hear those little contented sounds coming from them. Keep a pocket-sized photo album in your bag with pictures of family and friends. Take this out and focus on them for a few minutes and experience the feeling of well-being flow over you.

These are only a few examples of how easy it is to make your senses work as a powerful tool to distress in any situation where your emotions can erupt into anger and aggression. Look deeper at your own life and you will find even more ways to use your senses (Segal and Smith, 2019).

Emergency tick list for a reality check

This list can save you from the severe consequences of acting impulsively when you are in volatile situations. Print it out and keep it in your wallet, have a copy on your laptop and on your cell phone. When you feel anger starting to build, go over your reality check questions and answer them honestly.

- Is my anger justified in this specific situation or am I overreacting?
- Is the issue at hand really significant enough for me to lose my temper?
- Is there anything I can do within my power to change the state of affairs?
- Is taking action important enough to warrant the consequences of an eruption in anger?
- Is it worth my time to take any form of action in the present situation?
- What is the scale of importance of this issue when viewed in the complete picture?

Music

Music elicits an emotional response in people. It can make you happy, nostalgic, sad and even make you feel anger. Angry music is definitely a no-no when you are using music as an anger management coping strategy. What you need to do is find music that resonates with you and make you feel relaxed and happy. With a bit of experimenting, you can have a good playlist of music always on hand.

Use your playlist before you enter a situation that you know will be stressful, in order to prepare yourself to deal with the situation calmly and prevent your anger from spiking. Later, use music after the stressful event to tone down anxiety. Many people find music to be a great sleep therapy, so search for music that will lull you to sleep. Even if it is just one particular song, you can create a loop and let it run for several hours. A night of sound sleep is worth the search.

Find your inner Muse

We all have something we are passionate about. You don't have to be particularly good at it, you just need to enjoy doing it and find it fulfilling. It is your creative outlet, so this is not for anyone else's enjoyment. This is for you, and your physical enjoyment and mental well-being is all that counts.

The options are endless; some people enjoy pulling

out weeds and tending a perfect garden, while others like to paint or sculpt. You are the only one who knows what streak of creativity works for you, and that is what you must focus on.

Keep reminding yourself that the coping strategies you put in place now are the foundation stones you lay for a life where anger no longer rules you. This is a life of freedom, and you deserve to live it to the fullest extent. So don't make excuses of not having the time, or that you are no good at doing what you enjoy. You owe it to yourself to find your inner Muse.

Immediate, interim solutions for the situation

You need to have strategies in place for fast, immediate solutions to prevent you from an angry blowup. These solutions are not permanent or long-term. These are for coping in the moment.

You get home after a tiring day and the kids have turned your study into a playroom. Of course, you are angry because your study is in a mess. Losing your temper is not going to undo the mess. Instead, it will just create more problems and stress in the family. Turn around, walk out of the study and firmly close the door. Out of sight, out of mind. Go and distress and you can deal with the situation later in a much better frame of mind.

This is only one scenario, but this type of situation

pops up at home, at work, and in social settings. You need to do your homework and think about all the various situations you have encountered where a temporary solution and some time to calm down would have resulted in a positive outcome. Make a list and then start a column for possible immediate solutions to each situation. This list will come in handy in the future.

For your eyes-only letters

When you are so angry that you simply need to vent, yet logical enough to know that confronting the person who made you so angry would end badly or have consequences you do not want, write a letter. Grab a pen and start writing or hit the keyboard and type away. Vent all you want, tell the person exactly why you think he or she acted like an idiot or some other interesting description. When you have finished, either delete it or tear up the letter.

The physical act of putting words to the emotions you are feeling is liberating. You get to express exactly how you are feeling and by doing so, you dump stress and anger. At the same time, you have perfectly managed your anger without harming a relationship or brought more stress and anxiety into your home, workplace, or social environment.

Start a pampering routine

Pampering is not only for women- guys are entitled to

pampering, too! This is another coping mechanism that puts you first. The emphasis here is on routine, so make this part of your daily, weekly or monthly routines.

The choice of pampering is entirely personal and must be something that makes you feel physically and emotionally relaxed and happy. Getting a pedicure, a head massage and a haircut, or going for a regular chiropractic session are all possibilities. Remember, this is your time and your coping strategy, and you will gain the benefits.

Laughter

Laughter truly is the best medicine. It actually has many physical health benefits that we never really think about.

Laughing improves your physical health by reducing stress hormones and boosting your immune system, as well as acting as a muscle relaxant that in turn improves your heart health. As you laugh, your body releases endorphins, the feel-good hormone, which greatly benefits your emotional well-being.

Make a conscious effort to bring joy into your day and look for things that will make you laugh. Take a few minutes to play silly games with the dog, spent some time looking at a joke website or watch some comedy shows, or catch up with close friends (Holland, 2019).

Channel angry energy

Anger produces energy, which is why you are so restless when you are angry. Instead of wasting that energy brooding about what made you angry, or the situation that frustrates you, channel that extra energy into doing something productive.

We all have a to-do list we are ignoring as best we can. This is the perfect time to pull out that list and get busy. Tackle that storeroom your partner has threatened to set alight because it's in shambles, or start that DIY project you know you should have done ages ago. A bonus is that if you pour this energy into tasks that are physically challenging, you are getting exercise too.

Another way to use this energy is to step away from thinking only about how to use it for day-to-day personal matters. Instead, join a group that promotes a cause you care about, such as a clean environment, and pour your energy into organizing rallies to promote awareness. Another good option is to join a group that works toward making positive changes to society, like a volunteer club.

Whatever form of productivity you choose, it means you focus on doing something positive and you do not dwell on whatever angered you. You can get inventive with a list of things to do when you have angry energy to burn.

Avoid alcohol and recreational drugs

Alcohol and recreational drugs are a definite no-no. We have discussed how both of these are unhealthy quick fixes that do not solve any of your underlying anger issues. It is important enough to add these to your list of coping strategies as both of these substances can have a devastating effect on your life in general. They will set you back in your goal of becoming free of uncontrolled emotions.

Your support system is crucial here as it is so easy to grab that quick fix in situations of extreme stress. Have a serious talk with people in your life that you trust, including family and friends, but also those in your work environment. You need their active support, and while it is possible that you will at times resent their interference, it is for the best. These feelings will fade as you can see the progress you make in anger management and your support system will stay with you for the long-haul. Remember, they know you having emotional problems and they are affected by this as well; they want you to succeed just as much as you do.

Pressure point massage

Acupressure and reflexology have been practiced for thousands of years to relieve pain, stress, anger, and anxiety. Combined, they are an excellent anger management strategy that brings you instant relief.

Of course, going for professional acupressure sessions are amazing and if you have access to them, make use of this. However, with our hectic pace of living and our need to always be on the go, it is not always possible to stop in for a session.

Invest the time into finding video tutorials that will teach you the basic acupressure points focused on relieving anger and anxiety. The technique is easy to learn, and once you have this skill, it is yours for life. Pressure point massage brings a wide range of benefits and you can do it anywhere and need no special equipment.

One of the symptoms of poor anger control is insomnia. This can be addressed with an acupressure massage. The same pressure points that help you to sleep better also work for stress relief. Learning to do pressure point massage on yourself is worth your time as it has simply too many benefits to ignore as part of your anger management coping strategies.

Dump toxic routines

Routine is part of every human being's daily life. Without routines, chaos will rule. The problem is that certain routines might turn your day from smooth and calm into a rollercoaster of emotion.

Think about your days and notice if you have red flags waving about a certain aspect, whether it is getting to work and being stuck in traffic at the same places daily, never getting a hot cup of coffee when you want it, or navigating school drop-offs for your kids. We all have these toxic routines and now it is time to permanently do something about them. The simple answer to this problem is to change your routine.

Find another route to work, even if the new route is longer. It is worth it to arrive at work without wanting to bite the head off of the receptionist who innocently greets you with a smile.

If you want hot coffee on tap and the machine is always empty when you get there, invest in a flask. This is a simple, easy solution that solves your problem and benefits everyone else as they become less stressed around you.

Kids will always need to be taken to school or dropped off at daycare. If this is a stumbling block in your anger management, speak to other parents and organize a lift club or put an advertisement on the school bulletin board.

These are a few examples of toxic routines that turn your day from tranquil to filled with annoyance and frustration. Find the best solution for each of the toxic routines you have, because with every toxic routine you eliminate, you move closer to your goal. Visualize a pie chart of your toxic routines and imagine each block turn from angry red to tranquil and stress-free blue.

Communicate your anger

This does not mean having a spectacular explosion of anger, yelling and waving your arms like an operatic diva. This will not truly express why you are angry. Do not try to convey your message in the heat of the moment. You need to calm down first. Only then will you be able to speak without your emotions overruling your message. Get a trusted friend to help you with this, and practice until you get to the point where you are capable of a dialogue that is calm, mature and rational. A good tip when choosing a rehearsal partner is to look for someone who is not emotionally involved with the situation.

Kids have time out, so can adults

Everyone knows that time out works great for kids, but adults can use this coping mechanism just as easily. Personal, intimate relationships are probably the most difficult to manage, and it can be challenging to diffuse conflict when locked in a confrontation with your partner. This is an aspect of anger management that is critical to control, because when your personal relationship falters, the other areas of your life tend to collapse in a domino effect.

Getting upset and angry with your partner is normal. We all do and say irritating things when our needs are not fully met. How you handle these instances will make or break the situation and this is where taking a time out is of the utmost importance.

You know you need that time out, but if you don't handle it correctly, you are going to keep battling with anger in your personal relationship with your partner. The emphasis here is on the word "partner." You need input and cooperation from your partner for this coping strategy to be successful.

Sit your partner down and discuss the need for a time out once both of you are calm. The time out rules and procedure must be agreed on by both partners and both of you must be comfortable with this.

Things to discuss are how long time out should be, as we are all different and some of us flare up in anger and just as quickly it fizzles out again, while some of us have slow-burn anger that builds up over time and takes a very long time to dissipate. If the time out period you both agree on is not sufficient, then adjust it. Agree on a pre-arranged signal so that you can alert your partner that you need to take time out when you feel the anger building up.

Time out is for you to allow your anger to cool down. You need to do something that will restore your emotions to a manageable level. Discuss activities with your partner, then when you go into time out, he or she will know you are going to listen to relaxing music, meditate, or go for a jog around the park. It is important that your partner knows the duration of the time out and what you will be doing, otherwise, they will feel anxious about how long you will be away and when your discussion can resume.

The final part of your time out therapy is discussing the issue that resulted in the time out. You cannot leave the reason for your anger unresolved. Time out will restore your equilibrium and allow you to discuss the issue in a rational manner (Salazar, 2015).

Don't play the blame game

Stop using general terms in conflict situations. This is not about 'you did this,' 'he is inconsiderate,' 'nobody shows me the respect I deserve,' or 'everybody does what they want.' These statements are the different ways you transfer blame for your anger onto other people, events, or circumstances.

Practice until every time you start to play the blame game, your inner alarm goes off to stop you. You are in charge of your anger issues and you are the only one who can take responsibility for your emotions and anger.

In history, the blame game has started wars and caused unhappiness for countless people. There is no need for you to keep being a statistic; by removing the blame game from the equation, you grow your self-awareness. You start thinking about what you really feel and how everything you say can influence the feelings of other people.

'I' statements

"I" statements are one of the best ways to deal with anger. Learn and practice to start your sentences with 'I am angry' or 'I am upset'. We very easily fall into the habit of starting off by saying, "You did this" or "She made me angry". Changing to 'I' statements works equally well at home and the workplace.

By using the correct opening statement, you immediately make yourself the focus. You are not pointing out shortcomings in another person or a company, therefore the other people involved will not be offended or get angry. The last thing needed in a tense situation is more frustration and anger, and by focusing on your own feelings, you turn the whole situation around and a positive dialogue can then follow. This is a long-term strategy that, once perfected, becomes a life-long approach to handling all types of stressful situations (Martin, 2013).

Develop and improve your listening skills

Of course, we all listen to what people say, but hearing the words people say does not mean you are actually listening actively to them.

To be able to listen actively, you must first remove certain behavior patterns and actions. Once you stop these negative actions, you can start growing your active listening skills.

When you are sitting there like a wooden carving you are not actively listening at all. People realize that you are not really taking in anything they are saying and this causes them to feel unworthy, resulting in unnecessary negativity.

Not allowing someone to finish their sentence before you interrupt is not only rude and distracting, it clearly shows that you are not listening and that you think that whatever you want to say is more important. Interrupting and abruptly changing the subject in mid-conversation clearly shows that you have not been actively listening.

Stop being critical of what people are talking about or interrupting them with critical responses and going into lecture mode. This immediately brings heated emotions into the conversation. People feel humiliated when you take over their ideas and make them look bad. This negative behavior is especially rude in a work environment and it reflects back on you as being aggressive and having no empathy.

Nothing upsets a person more than when you start giving them unsolicited advice. Make sure before you advise anyone that they actually want advice from you and that the advice you are about to give is factually correct.

To be able to develop good listening skills, you will first have to make a conscious effort to stop any of these bad listening skills. With practice it is possible, and as you move away from the aforementioned negative listening habits, you will be able to be an active listening partner in a conversation. Your mind will no longer be preoccupied with other thoughts and you won't be waiting to interrupt with your own input. Instead, you will be able to show empathy to the speaker and their message (Marslew, 2011).

Rehearsal and Roleplay

You are the main performer in this play of gaining emotional freedom through anger management. We all know that any Broadway play takes a lot of rehearsal and it does not fall into place all at once. This means that rehearsal and roleplay will be powerful coping strategies that you will use in all the different areas of your life.

Make notes of what triggers you into angry emotional outbursts. Then look at different options of how you can prevent outbursts such as these. Rehearsals give you the opportunity to work through the options of what to say and do in specific circumstances and events where your emotions cannot be easily controlled.

By role-playing and rehearsing the different scenarios with several positive outcomes, you will be able to stop and take a breath in situations where your anger may escalate. You will have an action plan ready and not impulsively get triggered into a display of anger.

You can take rehearsal and role-play a step further by involving someone you trust and feel comfortable with. That person can act as your antagonist and you can try to devise solutions to prevent yourself from giving in to anger (Holland, 2019).

CHAPTER SIX

EMOTIONAL COPING STRATEGIES

E motional coping mechanisms go hand in hand with practical coping mechanisms to make positive changes to your life and managing your anger issues. Most of the practical coping mechanisms work as a two-way street, involving physical coping mechanisms that bring emotional benefits.

Relaxation apps

Technology really has some amazing benefits. We carry our cell phones with us wherever we go, so put yours to use in managing your anger and to destress.

There are so many apps available that it can seem daunting at first to find one that is the right fit for your specific needs and that can help you cope with your anger issues. With a little patience and by trying out different kinds, you will be able to find plenty of great options.

Think of it as your own pocket therapist that is on-call 24/7.

Personal mantras

Create a personal mantra to use in moments of extreme stress or anger, or when you need to stop and refocus before you give in to impulsive actions. This mantra is especially helpful if other options of distressing are not available right away. It can be a single word such as 'chill' or 'relax' or a phrase that has a special meaning that will stop your emotions from careening off the tracks like a runaway express train.

Add visualization for an extra boost to your mantra. Should you choose a phrase from your favorite childhood book, for instance, add a visual from the book as you repeat your mantra to help bring your emotions under control faster.

One of the most poignant songs of all time is the song "Let It Be," by The Beatles. It still has as much impact on people today as it did when it was released nearly 50 years ago. Take a phrase from this song as your personal mantra and you will find that it works wonders to bring your emotions to a place of calm.

Keep an emotions journal

It is not easy for everyone to verbalize their feelings. Some people actually find it stressful to talk about their emotions. Your emotions journal is private, for your eyes only, so you can feel comfortable expressing the emotions that you experience in different circumstances.

The act of writing your emotions down can have a calming effect on you. You will then find it easier to examine and re-evaluate the circumstances of a particular event that lead to an emotional and angry outburst and make notes of how you would have preferred to respond in that situation. These notes will guide you in the future as you deal with similar events, this time in a calmer and more rational manner. Think about your emotions journal as a stepping stone that carries you along towards healthy emotional well-being.

Grudges

Grudges are easy to hold onto; people dwell on them when they have been hurt until there is no room for anything positive. When you have been hurt or wronged by another person, you do not want to be taken advantage of again. We would rather hold on to resentment and negative feelings like a suit of armor, and not allow anyone to hurt us again.

Carrying grudges pushes up your stress levels, and living with a high level of stress hormones has a serious impact on your physical health and your emotional well-being (Johnson, 2006).

The cost of holding grudges

When you cannot let go you carry this anger and resentment, you bring it into every relationship you have, from work to family life. Carrying this extra baggage around with you tends to sour your outlook on life and take away your ability to enjoy all the little things that should make you happy. People don't like to be around a person who is constantly negative, as this attitude lessens their enjoyment in experiences, and people are likely to distance themselves from you. Make a conscious decision to let go of grudges. If at first you find this difficult, simply keep going. Progress in baby steps, and each time you succeed in letting go of a grudge, remember that it is an achievement to be proud of.

Gratitude

No matter how angry and stressed out you are, there are many things you have in your life to be grateful for. We just tend to forget those things when we are emotionally overloaded.

Being thankful for what you have in your life is not

about how many material possessions you have and how large your bank balance is. Some of the most affluent people are not very happy at all. It is about the worth you attach to each thing you have in your life.

Do not make the common mistake of underestimating the value of gratitude as a coping strategy. When you practice gratitude on a regular basis, you reap immediate benefits when you encounter an emotionally stressful situation. However, many people are not aware of the long-term benefits that could be theirs.

It has come to light through studies into positive psychology that when actively practicing gratitude on a regular basis, it brings changes to your life that you might not expect.

The studies have found that you have a greatly heightened awareness regarding your mental and physical wellness. The result is that you start taking better care of your body and mind. You choose to eat healthier and make sure that you have regular medical and dental check-ups, ensuring a better quality of life.

Your outlook on life becomes more optimistic and you find happiness in many things you hardly noticed before. Your mental alertness improves, as well as your ability to cope with the many demanding situations of daily living.

To assist you in making it easier to practice gratitude

on a daily basis, it is helpful to keep a gratitude journal. Take a few minutes each day and think about what you have to be thankful for in general and also specifically for that day (Madell, 2017).

Emotional lifeline

We have discussed how important your support system is as you learn to take control of your anger issues and build your skills in dealing with your uncontrolled emotions. You need to establish an emotional lifeline within that support system. Who that person will be will depend on you. It must be someone that you literally trust with your life. That one special person that you can reach out to in times of crisis, who will be there for you no matter what.

There can be no secrets between you and your emotional lifeline, no hogwash, no playing mind games. This is the person you need to turn to in times of intense emotional stress and know that this person will stand by you, talk you down from an impending meltdown and guide you until you can implement other emotional coping strategies that you have in place.

Putting an emotional lifeline in place does not imply that you are weak or powerless to manage your anger issues. It means that you are human and serious about anger management and mature enough to reach out in times of crisis.

Do something good

To do something good for someone without expecting anything in return, no gains or acknowledgment, will allow you to receive the greatest reward possible. You add a boost to your mental well-being. The feeling of liking yourself is a crucial emotional coping mechanism.

You do not have to spend money or make any other investment except your time. If you are not comfortable doing a random act of kindness, start small. When you see a person struggling with bags of groceries in the parking lot, go and lend a helping hand. Walk them to their car and chat with them.

You immediately take your mind off the stress you are under and you stop dwelling on why you are angry. Your mind completely refocuses on the here and now, and in the process, you help another human being. The simple act of lending a helping hand with a smile also contributes to their own mental well-being, as they probably were frustrated with their inability to manage their bags. Your anger coping mechanism becomes a snowball and enhances the life of another person at the same time that you are diffusing your feelings of anger.

When you engage your mind in this way, your own emotions are no longer the focal point. You see the world with wide-open eyes and are more in tune with the feelings of those around you. You may even find that an activity that started as an emotional coping strategy grows into new friendships as you become active in your community.

A mental sanctuary

Emotions are energy guzzlers. The more intense the emotion, the faster it depletes your store of energy. You need a place where you can recharge mentally. Ideally, if you have a space at home where you won't be disturbed, you can make this into your oasis. Create ambiance and tranquility in your sanctuary where you can relax, recharge and simply allow all the feelings of stress, anxiety and anger to drain away.

Create an extra level of tranquility by involving your sense of smell. Burn candles with your favorite fragrance or incense. Aromatherapy oil burners work as well to add a sensory element. By doing this, you will associate your favorite smell with feelings of tranquility, contentment, relaxation, and safety.

Visualization is important as part of this emotional coping strategy. Sit or lie comfortably and form a picture in your mind of a place of complete relaxation. Concentrate and focus on specific aspects of this place, such as seeing the branches of a tree gently swaying in the breeze or hearing water flowing in a stream.

You can recreate your sanctuary when you are not at

home by finding a quiet, empty room and closing your eyes. Visualize your place of tranquility. This will allow you to calm your mind in the middle of a situation filled with anger. To help you balance your emotions even faster, carry your favorite scent with you on a cloth or a sachet in a pocket or your bag.

Mood charts

Not everyone finds it easy to track their emotions and to pinpoint what exactly caused them to experience a specific emotion. Our days are busy and we have a million things to remember, and while still trying to make time for ourselves. So it's not surprising that we don't pick up on those first warning signs of a change in our emotions.

To assist you in managing your anger, it's back to school and doing homework. You need to create two charts: a daily mood chart and a weekly mood chart. You can download templates from the internet and customize them to suit your needs.

Your daily chart should have lines to track your emotions every two hours and columns for your basic feelings such as sadness, anger, happiness, stress, anxiety, excitement and physical fatigue, as well as space to make notes.

Doing mood charts will allow you to you reflect on your day, and understand why certain emotions spiked, where you were when it happened and under what circumstances or in what situations these emotions tend to get triggered. In a short while, you will have a visual guide that shows you where, when and in what situations you experience emotional wobbles.

A weekly mood chart works on the same basis as a daily one: tracking at two-hour intervals with columns for each day of the week. Patterns will show up that quickly alert you to stumbling blocks. If they occur at regular intervals, it may mean that you need to change your routine ("Daily Mood Chart",2013)

CHAPTER SEVEN

OUTSIDE THE BOX COPING STRATEGIES

Y ou can never have too many strategies to deal with your anger issues. In fact, the more, the merrier. Bringing a playful element to your strategies will allow you to break away from the norm and have some child-like fun.

Remember, these are your anger issues, these are your coping strategies and if acting a little bit silly works and makes you laugh, it's worth it.

Smack that anger right out of you

There is something incredibly satisfying about hitting a ball. When it comes to emotional issues, you can literally smack all that anger out of your system. You can go play a game of racquetball or tennis, or invest in a punching bag if that will do the trick. Put a pole up in your backyard and when you feel your emotions getting out of control, go and smack that ball. This is a great way to get rid of anger without getting into trouble with the law, with the added bonus of getting a physical workout at the same time.

Empty chair therapy

Some therapists use what is called Gestalt therapy. You can do this on your own as a coping strategy. Place two chairs in a room and sit on one. The empty chair is for the person you are angry with.

This is a great form of role-playing therapy and this gives you the opportunity to express all the anger you have towards this person in a safe environment. You can be as impolite as you want to be and really have a good go at the person that is the focus of your anger. So let it rip, the empty chair has no feelings you can hurt, nor will the chair be offended.

Pop bubbles

We all are quite familiar with the feeling of absolute joy as you pop a sheet of bubble wrap. It truly gives a feeling of being a naughty child doing something forbidden.

This is a simple coping strategy with huge benefits. Visualize a piece of anger or frustration fading away with each bubble that you pop. Squishing anger to death can be a lot of fun (Tatakovsky, 2018).

Paper therapy

Get a pack of construction paper to keep handy. When you find it difficult to control your emotions, grab your pack of paper. Think about the feelings you are experiencing at that moment and decide which of the colors relate best to whatever it is you are feeling.

Visualize each piece of paper as the emotion you are struggling with, and pretend that as you rip up the paper, you are ripping that emotion to shreds.

Bubble popping and paper shredding are two of the best tactile coping strategies to help you when your emotions threaten to hijack your ability to deal with anger.

Mirror, mirror on the wall

Get a pocket mirror to keep with you. When you feel your emotions racing out of control take out your mirror and look at your face. Then imagine the worst expressions possible to show how exactly how angry you are at that moment. How long you keep this up is your decision. You will know when it has worked when you feel much calmer or you can't stop laughing at the faces you pull.

A word of advice: do not attempt this therapy in a

crowded restaurant or when seated in a meeting. This is best done where you can be alone or the unforeseen result may be that you will be carted off to the nearest loony bin before you have a chance to explain that you were doing anger management therapy.

Sing

Singing gives voice to your angry emotions, allowing you to express vocally what you are feeling inside. Do a quick Google search for songs expressing anger and you will immediately have an excellent list to choose from.

It does not matter how good or how bad your singing voice is, this is about vocalizing your anger. You can also create your own song and lyrics if that works better for you. You can use song therapy even at times where you can't sing out loud, by humming the song or just hearing the song in your mind.

Dreamcatcher of gratitude

Borrow from the Native American culture and use a dreamcatcher protection charm. Make your own dreamcatcher or buy one, there are many options to choose from.

Your dreamcatcher will become your visual gratitude journal as you pin slips of paper onto the web with things that you are grateful for. You can list everyone you love and care about, things that bring joy to your life or the things that give you the strength to face challenges.

The physical act of pinning the slips of paper to the web is therapeutic, and you can keep adding when you find something new to add to your visual gratitude journal.

Dance and stamp your feet

Music, rhythm, and dancing are as old as time and people have been portraying emotions through dance throughout human history. You do not have to be a flamenco dancer; it does not matter if you have two left feet and consider yourself a klutz.

Use dancing to express your emotions and get rid of all the negative feelings you have experienced during the day. As you move and stamp your feet, you are stamping on anger and the reasons that frustrated you. Literally, dance your anger away and if you can make this a daily routine, even better (Gilbert, 2018).

A hug buddy

Having a hug buddy when you are emotionally drained works wonders. You may have a soft toy from your childhood tucked away somewhere, or you can have a look at the amazing soft toys available today.

Many people have more than one hug buddy, and you will be glad for the company when you can't sleep or anxiety wears you down. Pack your hug buddy in when you go traveling; it will surprise you to know how many people do that. A hug buddy and traveling companion are just what the doctor ordered as a soft, cuddly coping mechanism in your anger management program.

Draw caricatures

Some of us paint, sketch, or sculpt to help us cope when emotions and situations are volatile. Not everyone is drawn to these activities, so start drawing caricatures instead.

Let your imagination take over and draw a wicked cartoon of the sour apple HR person in the company who seems to make it his task each day to annoy people. Dress him in a pink tutu and a unicorn hat if that will make you feel better, or visualize your CEO wearing a diaper and sucking his thumb.

Drawing caricatures will have you feeling much less stressed, and anger does not stand a chance against laughter.

CHAPTER EIGHT

WHAT DO YOU HAVE TO LOSE?

This is one of the most important questions to ask yourself and you should think honestly about your answer. This will determine how serious you are to be free from constant, uncontrolled emotions.

The best way for you to come to the answer is to draw up a balance sheet of your life. One column detailing where you are right now, and the other column of where you choose to be, detailing everything you can achieve with anger management, self-control, and healthy emotional intelligence. This balance sheet must include your personal life with family and friends, your career and workplace, and your social life.

It is a huge eye-opener once you start working on this balance sheet. It is not always the most comfortable exercise to do as, facing the reality of what your life has become through uncontrolled emotions can be disheartening. If this happens, it is the perfect moment to have a time-out. Walk away and allow your brain to be soothed, and then come back and see the incredible benefits you are achieving as you take each step forward on this journey to become who you choose to be.

Update your balance sheet regularly as you reach mileposts along the way. This way you can see how your life changes for the better.

You have so much to lose: all the anger, negativity, anxiety and destructive behavior. You stand to lose your isolation from everyone at home, at work and at play.

It really is all about having the best possible quality of life and freedom from the anger issues that are taking their toll on your health and emotional well-being.

CONCLUSION

You have now reached the point where you have all the knowledge about the elements of emotional intelligence and how to apply it to your life. The strategies detailed in this book are not difficult to come to grips with, and you can implement them with practice and perseverance. You have kept at it and reached this point, which indicates that you really want to make positive changes in your life and are totally fed up with being jerked around by your out of control emotions like an unwilling puppet on a string.

It is important to always keep in mind that while

making these much-needed and life-altering changes that asking for help from family and friends is not a show of weakness. Nobody is going to laugh at you or think you are being stupid. Everyone in your life is aware that you have anger issues and will assist where they can. They will encourage you and stand with you, for they want to see you get your emotions under control. The stronger your support system, the easier the whole transition will be from uncontrolled emotions to living your life as you are meant to.

Anger management is a bumpy road but it is absolutely worth it to travel on it. On the days you encounter bumps, keep repeating to yourself that emotional slavery has been abolished. Then dance and stamp your feet while singing loudly, "Snip, the cords are cut, the puppet show is over, this is my life, my choice."

REFERENCES

Bradbury, T. & Greaves, J. (2005). The emotional quick book. New York, NY: Simon & Shuster.

Goleman, D. (1996). Emotional intelligence: Why it can matter more than IQ. New Delhi, Delhi: Bloomsbury Publishing India Private Limited.

Smith, A. (June 6, 2022). 5 Ways to Showcase Your Emotional Intelligence as a Leader. Retrieved from https://aboutleaders.com/emotional-intelligence-leader/

Santos-Longhurst, A. (September 9, 2021). Do I have anger issues? How to identify and treat an angry outlook. Retrieved from https://www.healthline.com/health/anger-issues

Printed in Great Britain
by Amazon

21538431R00068